JACK BRADFIELD

Jack Bradfield is an award-winning writer and director. He is Artistic Director of Poltergeist, and recipient of the RTST Sir Peter Hall Director Award 2023. For Poltergeist, Jack has written and directed *Alice in Wonderland* (Brixton House, seven Offie Award nominations); *Ghost Walk* (New Diorama); *Art Heist* (New Diorama, London/Underbelly, Edinburgh/ HOME, Manchester/UK tour; Untapped Award 2019/Fringe Sell-Out Show/*Guardian* – Best Shows of the Fringe); *Lights Over Tesco Car Park* (Samuel French New Play Award/Fringe Sell-Out Show). As director: *Abigail's Party* (Northern Stage/ Rose Theatre). He is currently developing feature film and television projects.

Other Titles in this Series

Annie Baker
THE ANTIPODES
THE FLICK
INFINITE LIFE
JOHN

Mike Bartlett
THE 47TH
ALBION
BULL
GAME
AN INTERVENTION
KING CHARLES III
MIKE BARTLETT PLAYS: TWO
MRS DELGADO
SCANDALTOWN
SNOWFLAKE
UNICORN
VASSA *after* Gorky
WILD

Sonali Bhattacharyya
CHASING HARES
KING TROLL (THE FAWN)
LIBERATION SQUARES
TWO BILLION BEATS

Jez Butterworth
THE FERRYMAN
THE HILLS OF CALIFORNIA
JERUSALEM
JEZ BUTTERWORTH PLAYS: ONE
JEZ BUTTERWORTH PLAYS: TWO
MOJO
THE NIGHT HERON
PARLOUR SONG
THE RIVER
THE WINTERLING

Mohamed-Zain Dada
BLUE MIST
DIZZY

Lucy Kirkwood
BEAUTY AND THE BEAST
  with Katie Mitchell
BLOODY WIMMIN
THE CHILDREN
CHIMERICA
HEDDA *after* Ibsen
THE HUMAN BODY
IT FELT EMPTY WHEN THE HEART
  WENT AT FIRST BUT IT IS
  ALRIGHT NOW
LUCY KIRKWOOD PLAYS: ONE
MOSQUITOES
NSFW
RAPTURE
TINDERBOX
THE WELKIN

Stewart Pringle
THE BOUNDS
TRESTLE

Sam Steiner
KANYE THE FIRST
LEMONS LEMONS LEMONS LEMONS
  LEMONS
A TABLE TENNIS PLAY
YOU STUPID DARKNESS!

Jack Thorne
2ND MAY 1997
AFTER LIFE *after* Hirokazu Kore-eda
BUNNY
BURYING YOUR BROTHER IN
  THE PAVEMENT
A CHRISTMAS CAROL *after* Dickens
THE END OF HISTORY…
HOPE
JACK THORNE PLAYS: ONE
JACK THORNE PLAYS: TWO
JUNKYARD
LET THE RIGHT ONE IN
  after John Ajvide Lindqvist
THE MOTIVE AND THE CUE
MYDIDAE
THE SOLID LIFE OF SUGAR WATER
STACY & FANNY AND FAGGOT
WHEN WINSTON WENT TO WAR WITH
  THE WIRELESS
WHEN YOU CURE ME
WOYZECK *after* Büchner

Eleanor Tindall
TENDER

debbie tucker green
BORN BAD
DEBBIE TUCKER GREEN PLAYS: ONE
DIRTY BUTTERFLY
EAR FOR EYE
HANG
NUT
A PROFOUNDLY AFFECTIONATE,
  PASSIONATE DEVOTION TO SOMEONE
  (– NOUN)
RANDOM
STONING MARY
TRADE & GENERATIONS
TRUTH AND RECONCILIATION

Phoebe Waller-Bridge
FLEABAG

Tom Wells
BIG BIG SKY
BROKEN BISCUITS
DRIP *with* Matthew Robins
FOLK
JUMPERS FOR GOALPOSTS
THE KITCHEN SINK
ME, AS A PENGUIN
STUFF

Ross Willis
WOLFIE
WONDER BOY

Jack Bradfield

THE HABITS

NICK HERN BOOKS
London
www.nickhernbooks.co.uk

A Nick Hern Book

The Habits first published in Great Britain as a paperback original in 2025 by Nick Hern Books Limited, The Glasshouse, 49a Goldhawk Road, London W12 8QP

The Habits copyright © 2025 Jack Bradfield

Jack Bradfield has asserted his right to be identified as the author of this work

Cover photography: Dwi Yulianto/Shutterstock

Designed and typeset by Nick Hern Books, London
Printed in Great Britain by Mimeo Ltd, Huntingdon, Cambridgeshire PE29 6XX

A CIP catalogue record for this book is available from the British Library

ISBN 978 1 83904 400 7

CAUTION All rights whatsoever in this play are strictly reserved. Requests to reproduce the text in whole or in part should be addressed to the publisher.

Amateur Performing Rights Applications for performance, including readings and excerpts, by amateurs in the English language should be addressed to the Performing Rights Department, Nick Hern Books, The Glasshouse, 49a Goldhawk Road, London W12 8QP, *tel* +44 (0)20 8749 4953, *email* rights@nickhernbooks.co.uk, except as follows:

Australia: ORiGiN Theatrical, tel +61 (2) 8514 5201,
email enquiries@originmusic.com.au, web www.origintheatrical.com.au

New Zealand: Play Bureau, 20 Rua Street, Mangapapa, Gisborne 4010,
tel +64 21 258 3998, email info@playbureau.com

Professional Performing Rights Applications for performance by professionals in any medium and in any language throughout the world should be addressed to Independent Talent Group Ltd, 40 Whitfield Street, London W1T 2RH, *tel* +44 (020) 7636 6565

No performance of any kind may be given unless a licence has been obtained. Applications should be made before rehearsals begin. Publication of this play does not necessarily indicate its availability for performance.

www.nickhernbooks.co.uk/environmental-policy

Nick Hern Books' authorised representative in the EU is
Easy Access System Europe – Mustamäe tee 50, 10621 Tallinn, Estonia
email gpsr.requests@easproject.com

For Mum

The Habits was first performed at Hampstead Theatre Downstairs, London, on 28 February 2025, with the following cast:

BEV	Debra Baker
JAMIE	Jamie Bisping
JESS	Ruby Stokes
MARYN	Sara Hazemi
DENNIS	Paul Thornley
Director	Ed Madden
Designer	Alys Whitehead
Lighting Designer	Laura Howard
Sound Designer	Max Pappenheim

Thanks

I'd like to thank everyone who has read, noted, supported (and inspired) this play.

Jessie Anand, Jamie Armitage, Heather Barr, Sally Bayley, Tom Brennan, Jon Brittain, David Byrne, Anushka Chakravarti, Emily Davis, Oli Forsyth, Rosa Garland, Dennis Harrison, Robert Icke, Penny Layden, Fergus Macdonald, Ed Madden, John Marquez, Will Merrick, Amy Perkis, Charles Pigeon, Julia Pilkington, Kirsty Rider, Guy Sanders, Jessica Stewart, Will Spence, Finlay Stroud, Lyndsey Turner, and Kieran Smith, whom we miss very much.

J.B.

Foreword
Ed Madden, director

At the end of our first week of rehearsals for *The Habits,* Jack and the cast and I visited an immersive tabletop gaming café in Shoreditch, and played a session of Dungeons & Dragons as a company. Jack was the only one of our number to have played before; though the rest of us had done our research and watched many (many) hours of both casual and professional play online, we hadn't had the experience of clutching our own character sheets and twenty-sided dice and waiting for a charismatic Dungeon Master to lead us on an adventure.

It was an entirely eye-opening afternoon. Quite apart from learning how different it feels to play D&D than one might expect from watching it being played, I was fascinated by the social dynamic of the game and its relationship to that of the rehearsal room. They share, among much else, the trying on of new roles; the forging of a cooperative methodology; and the vital necessity of trust as the bedrock of collaborative creative endeavour, since nothing is so stifling as the fear that there are *wrong answers* by which one might be shamed. Best of all, they share a special mix of seriousness and larkiness – enough of the former to hold taut the fabric of a shared imaginative world, and of the latter to foster the conditions (amity, relaxation, playfulness) that make the work possible.

The other fascinating thing was watching Jack. At a crucial juncture, our adventurers came into possession of a map which promised to lead us to the object of our mission, but Jack, in the role of a zealous cleric, made a play to *destroy* the map – divine providence would guide us! It was a lightbulb moment. As the rest of us clung to the narrative scaffold of the quest, Jack embodied an understanding that D&D is a game of *character*; that story is shaped by behaviour. It is that understanding which fuels this play, and from which it derives its richness, humour, and compassion. It's a play about what it means to make decisions, and how those decisions coalesce into who we are; about what it means to build something with other people, and how that 'something' can acquire a life of its own.

Johan Huizinga wrote that 'all play moves and has its being within a play-ground marked off beforehand' and that all such play-grounds are 'temporary worlds within the ordinary world, dedicated to the performance of an act apart'. *The Habits* is set on the scuffed touchline; at the very edge of the card table; in the gloaming half-light where fantasy and reality blur.

February 2025

For fantasy is true, of course. It isn't factual, but it's true.
Ursula K. Le Guin

Characters

JESS, *sixteen*
MARYN, *twenty-one*
MILO, *twenty-one*
DENNIS, *fity-five*
BEV, *fifty*

A Note on the Text

This play takes place around a single table in WarBoar Boardgames Café, Bromley, BR1.

A forward slash in a line of dialogue (/) marks the point of interruption of overlapping dialogue. A forward slash at the beginning of a line of dialogue indicates that this line should begin before the previous has been completed.

[Text in square brackets indicates a words the character intends to say, but doesn't manage to.]

In this play, characters play Dungeons & Dragons. You can find an overview of the game online. Rules have been largely followed, with some small changes to support the dramatic action.

When characters are voicing a character in the game, their dialogue is written in this font.

This text went to press before the end of rehearsals and so may differ slightly from the play as performed.

ACT ONE

Scene One

WarBoar Boardgames Café, Bromley.

JESS, MARYN and MILO are at a table.

JESS is sixteen. Year 11 uniform and a long coat. Short hair. Glasses. Buttons with logos: Doctor Who, Zelda, *etc.*

MARYN is twenty-one. Faux-fur coat over office attire. By her side, a canvas bag with a character from a popular anime on it.

MILO is twenty-one. Leather jacket with patches, a Mountain Goats T-Shirt, some small cuts around his eyebrows and on his forehead. Gothic tattoos. A piercing or two.

JESS is leading a game of Dungeons & Dragons. There is music playing out of her laptop, scoring the adventure. She clutches a leather notebook – her crib sheet.

Everyone makes their own sound effects.

JESS. The goblin leaps into the air and slashes you with his blade.

JESS then rolls a twenty-sided die.

Twelve.

MILO. Miss. I take a swing at him with my axe.

MILO rolls.

Fourteen, plus three, seventeen.

JESS. That's a hit.

MILO rolls an eight-sided die.

MILO. Seven Damage.

JESS. He's looking worse for wear. Spitting up blood, scrabbling away.

MARYN. I cast Entangle.

JESS. Strength check –

>JESS *rolls*.

Ten – plus three. Thirteen.

MARYN. Success.

JESS. Magical ropes whip out of your hands and wrap round his legs. He falls forward – his face slams into the mud.

MILO. I pick him up, and throw him against a rock.

>MILO *is crouched over the table, growling:*

What do we have here?

JESS (*hissing*). Leave me alone, human. The hills are mine.

MILO. I narrow in. Right in his face.
Tell us what you know about The Nightmare King.

JESS. I know *nothing* about the Nightmare King. Nothing at all!

MILO. The villagers say you know where he is.

JESS. He – he – he spits at you. Pfft.

MILO. I will tear your arms off and cook them in the fire. I love the taste of roast goblin.

JESS. Kill me, go on, do it. I hate this life. Hounded. Attacked on my own land. Make it end.

MILO. I draw my axe, and go into a Barbarian Rage.

(*To* JESS.) Okay I'm gonna roll Attack.

>MILO *shakes the dice in his hand* –

MARYN. No. Look. Can we – not.

MILO. What?

MARYN. Eat someone... I mean –

MILO. What do you want me to do, snog him?

MARYN. I think I'm just still uncomfortable with you playing a woman.

MILO. What? Why? You play a man.

MARYN. Yeah but my man's not a sex fantasy.

MILO. I am shocked.

JESS. Guys –

MILO. She is not a sex fantasy. Wren is a hot barbarian babe but that's just who she is.

MARYN. You're such a…

MILO. What –

MARYN. Nothing.

JESS. / Um.

MILO. Say it.

MARYN. Nothing, I'm not saying it.

JESS. What are you going to say… to the goblin?

DENNIS comes over with a tray of drinks. Lightly greying goatee, ponytail. WarBoar branded T-Shirt. Cargo shorts with lots of pockets. He's fifty-five.

DENNIS. Table one… Hot chocolate?

JESS. Oh. Me. Thanks.

DENNIS. Oat milk chai latte.

MARYN puts her hand up.

And a pale ale.

Did I see your ID, Milo?

MILO. *Dennis.*

DENNIS. It's the rules.

MILO. *I used to work here.*

DENNIS (*leaning in*). If I don't check yours then the Year 11 Wargames Society over there will start having a go at me for checking theirs, and next thing I know they'll be launching another offensive on the beer fridge.

MILO *gives in and shows* DENNIS *his provisional licence. He looks at* MILO, *looks at the card, hands it back and gives him the beer.*

There you go.

Shout if you need anything.

DENNIS *goes.* MILO *checks his phone.*

MILO. Shit.

JESS. What?

MILO. I've got a job interview in the morning and I haven't done any prep.

JESS. Where for?

MILO. Robert Dyas.
I know.

Beat.

And they moved into the old HMV. Which I'm pissed off about. Thinking about bringing it up.

MARYN (*concerned*). In the interview?

MILO. If you don't buy physical media you're not actually supporting artists.

MARYN. Please don't bring this up in the interview.

MILO. It's cultural suppression.

MARYN. There's no culture to suppress in Bromley.

MARYN. What about the Bowie tribute band?

JESS. We can go!

MILO. Not worth it, he's only got rights to '95 onwards.

MARYN's phone pings.

MARYN. Sorry, one sec.

MILO slides his phone over to JESS.

MILO. Wanna see a video of a flamingo pulling off its own head?

It plays a video.

So its neck is stuck in the fence, yeah? Trying to get out. And then. Wait for it.

Beat.

JESS. Oh my god. That's the worst thing I've ever seen.

MARYN slams her phone down.

MARYN. It's eight p.m., why do they think they can text me at eight p.m.?

MILO. Just quit.

MARYN. I can't quit. I'm on a track.

JESS. What's a track?

MARYN. Well in six months I'll be an Associate, and then basically any firm will hire me so...

MARYN's distracted by something away from the table.

He's staring at us again.

MILO. That's because he hates me.

JESS. *Please* tell me.

MARYN. He –

MILO. Maryn.

MARYN. He stole –

MILO. – borrowed –

MARYN. A bunch of Magic: The Gathering cards.

MILO. What! They're expensive!

JESS. Last year I spent like all of my pocket money on them.

MARYN. God... *pocket money*.

MILO. Oi – how was your date?

MARYN (*right back*). I didn't go on a date.

MILO. Really? I thought you –

MARYN. I didn't go on a date, what are you talking about?

JESS. It's okay if you went on a date.

MARYN. Just to try to get myself used to it –

JESS. You don't have to be worried about going on a date, you can go on a date.
How was your date? I'm gonna stop saying 'date'.

MARYN. She was twenty-six and the moment I sat down she immediately asked me what my star sign was and I said Sagittarius and after that – it was like – like something dramatically changed – and she had one drink and made up an excuse and left. That's the problem with being bisexual: you have to go out with lesbians.

Can we keep playing please?

JESS *gets her head back in the game*.

JESS. The goblin is tied up. Milo's about to cook him –

MARYN. Right well I'm going to talk to this goblin. I put my hand on his shoulder and cast Zone of Truth.

JESS. Charisma saving throw...

JESS *rolls*.

A Zone of Truth forms around you for ten metres wide. No one can tell a lie.

MARYN. Right...

ACT ONE, SCENE ONE

MARYN *closes her eyes. She focusses... clears her throat.*

Then in the voice of a wandering wizard:

MARYN. Goblin, what's your name?

JESS. Gorthalax.

MARYN. We are trying to ascertain the whereabouts of The Nightmare King. We believe the world is in great danger, and we could use your help, yes?

MILO. Oh my god just kill him.

MARYN. Let me talk to Gregalax.

JESS. Gorthalax –

MARYN. Gorthalax.
What do you know of the Nightmare King?

JESS. His name is whispered throughout this land, but I do not know him.

MARYN. Right. Well. The people in the village sent us. They said you are his... Associate.

JESS. They lie. They think I bring bad luck to the harvest – but it is the rains that are spoiling the crop, it is their poor farming that is spoiling the crop! The village set you on me to satisfy their hate, their lust for blood.

MARYN. And why do they blame you?

JESS. Because... I am a goblin.

Beat.

MARYN. Right well this is absolutely unacceptable isn't it. We're going back to the village.

MILO. Hold on.

MARYN. What?

MILO. Well the village said they'd pay us if we killed him.

MARYN. *He's being persecuted.*

MILO. I mean *yeah*, but I want to buy a shield.

MARYN. We'll get gold another way, won't we Jess?

JESS. You've got to make the choice with the information you're given.

MILO. Then we should obviously kill him.

MARYN. You're doing this to annoy me.

MILO. We've made a contract with the village so – anyone, anyone would think carefully before we break it.

MARYN. So it's money or people's lives is it?

MILO (*sighing*). Oh my fucking god.

MARYN. Wow. Okay.

MILO. Don't.

MARYN. Why are you being so arsey today?

MILO. *Because*.

MARYN. What?

JESS. / Um –

MILO. Because you're being sanctimonious about this fucking goblin.

MARYN. I'm not being / sanctimonious –

MILO. *I went to Cambridge and now I can tell everyone what to do.*

JESS. I'm sure there'll be more –

MILO. Jess – give me a moment –

JESS. Sorry.

MILO. I didn't mean to – it's just – a lot of hypocrisy coming from the corporate lawyer.

MARYN. I'm playing my character.

MILO. And I'm playing mine and I want to finish the contract.

ACT ONE, SCENE ONE   21

MARYN. When have you ever cared about fulfilling a contract?

MILO. Oi. *Oi.*

MARYN. / I didn't meant that.

MILO. I have applied for thirty-four jobs in the last three months, I have not got a single one – last week, last week, I interviewed at Bromley PC Repairs and they said – '*What experience do you have fixing phones and PCs?*' – and I said I have fixed my own phone, and my own laptop, and I got a seven in IT GCSE, and then I don't hear anything for a whole week, then on the way here tonight I'm walking... and look in the window and they've hired Kira – Kira from school whose parents are loaded, and who didn't even go to IT because she was always at recorder ensemble.

MARYN *pushes away from the table and gets up.*

And we know why she got it.

MARYN. Why?

MILO *points to his white skin, points to his dick.*

That's not why you're not getting jobs.

MILO. Why aren't I getting jobs?

MARYN. You're not getting jobs because of –

MILO. What?

MARYN. Because of *this*! This. This shit.

Beat.

Ugh. I was having fun.

MILO. What did I say? *What did I say?* I didn't say anything.

MARYN. Ugh.

MILO. *Stop doing that with your throat.*

JESS. Hang on Maryn, wait, we can change things around –

MARYN. Sorry. I've been sent loads of work for tomorrow and it's late, and –

JESS. That's cool, that's cool! I've got homework, so – no worries.

MILO. What on?

JESS. English Civil War.

MILO. Who with?

JESS. Ms Lowe.

MILO. Oh my god she was so fit.

MARYN. I'll see you next week, yeah?

JESS. Aye aye captain.

MARYN. Bye Milo.

MILO. Bye.

MARYN goes.

You know it just fucks me off. She's on like 40k, assisting on legal campaigns against working people – If I get food poisoning at a Zizzi's and tweet about it, it's *her* that's coming for me – and then what, suddenly tells me to stick up for a goblin.

JESS. I want you to argue – it's like *Star Trek*, you know, when there's aliens in trouble, but do you break the Prime Directive, or do you / abide by the rules of the Federation –

MILO. At school she was full Social Justice Warrior. There was this boy, Mo. Matt knew him as well. I don't know if he told you...

JESS. Oh. No. He didn't.

MILO. She and like some other girls cancelled him.

JESS. Why?

MILO. Ranked all the girls in the year by hotness on his Snap.

JESS. Oh. Haha.

MILO. The thing is, so did I, I just didn't put it on the internet.

Right I'm going to prep for this interview.

JESS. Okay – I'll prep for next week. I have this idea about – anyway, I won't spoil it. Good luck –

MILO *stops.*

MILO. You okay? I didn't mean to mention –

JESS. I'm fine!

MILO. How's Mum and Dad?

JESS. Not great, but, yeah. Everyone's fine. Me and Dad are rewatching *Lord of the Rings*.

MILO. My mum's such a bitch at the moment.
She's like a paintball gun pointed permanently at my dick.

Beat.

We will meet again, warrior.

JESS. Safe travels!

MILO *grabs his backpack, heads out, and picks up the phone:*

MILO. Mum. Hi. Can you research and print off everything you can about Robert Dyas...

MILO *goes.*

JESS *starts to pack up her stuff.* DENNIS *appears behind her.*

DENNIS. Er.

JESS *jumps.*

Sorry, didn't mean to scare you. You guys are the last out so I'm just locking up.

JESS. Oh, okay sorry.

DENNIS. I mean, take your time –

JESS. I'm just going.

DENNIS. No rush. You know Milo used to – [work here] – for a bit.

JESS. Yeah.

DENNIS. And you guys are his mates?

JESS. Mhm.

Beat.

DENNIS. I've been watching you.

JESS stops packing for a second.

Sorry – not like that. Just. Everyone else comes in here and plays flipping Monopoly. I haven't seen anyone playing...

JESS. D&D?

DENNIS. It's great isn't it.
You can almost *see it,* in your head, can't you.

JESS. We've only just started. Last few weeks. I'm still learning the systems – there's so many little things to [memorise] – um...

DENNIS. This place used to be completely for RPGs. Had all the maps, and mini-figs, modules, we'd run live play sessions, but – no take up, so... widened the net... board games, then did the coffee, and – but it's having a comeback, isn't it? D&D. Last few years.

JESS. Sort of.

DENNIS. No one comes here though, they go to the chain one in Brixton. Draughts. You know, like [*a beer*] but also like... [*chequers*].

What I wanted to say is, you know, thumbs up, keep the flag flying... I hope you're having a good game, and –

DENNIS's phone pings. He checks it.

– I'll see you around.

He's about to leave, but then –

JESS. If I scale an orc from level three to level five, do I have to increase armour class, or just attack?

DENNIS (*immediately*). You have to multiply it by its dexterity modifier.

JESS. Where's that?

DENNIS. Hang on, I've got the books in the store cupboard. You're playing fifth edition?

JESS. Yep.

JESS nods, DENNIS exits. JESS waits.

DENNIS reenters with D&D books.

DENNIS. Here we go...

Are we talking a Grey Orc or a Mountain Orc?

JESS. Not sure I just chose orc –

DENNIS. Well let's say Mountain Orc. At level five... you're looking at an armour class of thirteen.

JESS is looking over his shoulder.

JESS. What's 'aggressive' mean?

DENNIS. That means in battle, as a bonus action, it can move up toward any hostile creature that it can see within its movement range.

JESS. One sec.

JESS gets a sheet from her backpack and starts scribbling on it.

DENNIS. What weapons have you given it?

JESS. Mine has a greataxe –

DENNIS. Says here it can also have a javelin if you want?

JESS (*scribbling this down furiously*). Yes please.

DENNIS. For ranged attacks up to one hundred and twenty feet. Anyway. Borrow them.

JESS. Are you sure?

DENNIS. Yeah.

JESS packs the books into her bag.

Awkward pause.

DENNIS points to a dragon hanging above them.

There's only about five hundred of these in the world you know.

And probably only about four hundred people want one.

JESS puts on the dust jackets.

Dennis, by the way.

JESS. Jess.

JESS picks up her bag.

DENNIS. Well it was nice to meet you Jessica.

JESS. Nice to meet you too.

JESS walks to the door. DENNIS builds up to something. He does a voice:

DENNIS. *Who knows what adventures await?*

JESS. What?

DENNIS. It's nothing, it's something that I used to say to the customers when they came in...

Welcome to WarBoar. As you scramble through tombs, I will provide sustenance, as you battle monsters, I will bring you potions, and when you tire of your journey, I will offer up new worlds. Who knows what adventures await?

Beat.

JESS *(awkwardly)*. Yeah. Who knows?

Scene Two

JESS, MARYN, MILO *and* DENNIS *at the table.*

DENNIS *doing an Welsh accent, and strumming an acoustic guitar.*

DENNIS. Adventurers, warriors, citizens of Greyport – the drinks are on ME!

And then I keep strumming on my lute, and I play a jig for the whole tavern.

It's a – yeah – ha – it's a rude song. 'Shove your wand up your bum' or something like that –

JESS. Yep, okay, everyone's singing the popular tavern song, Shove Your Wand Up Your Bum.

DENNIS *finds this very funny.* MILO *and* MARYN *glance at each other.*

DENNIS. I go over to – Milo – and I clasp your hand.

Pleased to meet you warrior. Your name?

MILO. I am Wren, scourge of goblins, wielder of the great axe of Dalinar, last daughter of the Blood-Clan of Dark Moon.

DENNIS. Well met! I am Grimble, the dwarven bard. I adventure across the land singing songs of heroes and villains, battles and monsters, struggles and conflicts – as well as the odd tune for a rowdy tavern.

(*To Maryn.*) And you?

MARYN. Winglass.

DENNIS. Grimble gives you this grin and he's like: You're a wizard?

MARYN. Yes.

DENNIS. I find wizards fascinating creatures.

Beat.

Why so quiet?

JESS *gives* MARYN *a browned piece of paper.*

JESS. Map of the courthouse.

MILO. Grimble, we have reason to believe the magistrate is a secret zealot of *The Nightmare King.*

DENNIS. Guys – sorry – what's the Nightmare King?

MARYN, MILO *and* JESS, *from rote, at the same time:*

MARYN/MILO/JESS. *The Nightmare King, with eyes of flame,*
Beware his power, beware his name,
He waits within his cavern deep
To wrap the world in eternal sleep.

JESS. So, the rumour is that – far in the North – a prince was corrupted by the powers of Dark Magic. He surrendered himself to the Infernal Plane in return for immense power. His influence is growing.

DENNIS. And you want to stop him.

MARYN. Well he's evil, and it's a wizard's duty to keep the world in balance.

MILO. And Wren needs to prove she is *the greatest warrior of all time.*

DENNIS. Grimble's looking for the subject of a song. An epic ballad.

JESS (*loves that idea*). Putting *that* in the book.

She scribbles it down.

DENNIS. Right who wants what? Hot choc, pale ale, and…

MARYN *shakes her head.*

Sure?

MARYN *nods.*

Okay right back.

DENNIS *gets up and goes.*

MARYN (*whispering*). *Oh my god* –

JESS. What?

MARYN. Why didn't you tell us he was going to play!

JESS. We only decided last night. He texted –

MARYN. He *texted* you?

MILO. Wait are you not pro-Dennis?

MARYN. He's just. (*To* JESS.) He's not... [perving on you] is he?

JESS. What? No no no.

MARYN. *Okay* –

JESS. He's seeing someone anyway.

MILO. *He* has a girlfriend?

MARYN. Why do you know that?

JESS. No, he just mentioned he had a date or something.

MARYN. Why's he telling you about dates? *How long has this been going on?*

JESS. Three weeks.

MILO (*to* MARYN). *I think,* and don't take this the wrong way –

MARYN. You're going to say it's because I hate men.

MILO. You *do hate men*.

MARYN. Why are you suddenly pro-Dennis?

MILO. I'm just glad he's talking to me again.

JESS. He's...

MARYN. What?

JESS. He's *cool*.

MARYN. He wears cargo shorts and he doesn't / shower –

JESS. Stop talking about this *he's right there* –

MARYN. How long does someone have to stare at you across a room for you to think they're your friend?

JESS. We've been talking when you guys leave –

MARYN. Jess –

JESS. What?

MARYN. *Jess.*

JESS. It's my game. I want him to play, okay, I want him to play.

DENNIS *comes back with the drinks.*

DENNIS. A pint of ale for Wren!

MILO. Thank you dear Grimble!

DENNIS (*bowing to* JESS). And a hot chocolate for our kind and benevolent Dungeon Master.

JESS. Thank you very much.

DENNIS. Where were we?

JESS. You were planning to sneak into the courthouse.

JESS *slams her hands on the table.*

How are you going to do this?

MILO. I go into Barbarian Rage, walk in and gut all the guards with my blade.

MILO *mimes decimating a group of guards.*

MARYN. *No we're not* doing that. The map says there's a direct route to her office through the service entrance.

MILO. Am I ever going to get to go into Barbarian Rage? What is an eagle without its wings?

MARYN. Well I let you kill the cow last week.

MILO. That's not the same.

DENNIS. A cow?

MILO. It was judging me with its eyes.

JESS. Roll Stealth.

MILO. Okay...

MILO *picks up the dice.* MARYN *grabs it from him.*

MARYN. No, I'll do it, I have better Stealth.

DENNIS. I have the best Stealth, actually.

MARYN. Okay.

DENNIS *rolls.*

DENNIS. Sixteen plus three... nineteen.

JESS. This is a smooth entrance.

MILO. Fuck yes.

DENNIS. Okay so Grimble leaps up the drainpipe like a monkey, slips through the window completely unseen, and lowers a rope for you guys.

MARYN. We climb up.

JESS. You collapse into a corridor on the top floor. At the end of the corridor there's a guard. He hasn't seen you yet, but he's about to turn...

MARYN. Fuck – er – I cast Sleep.

MARYN *rolls.*

Shit, seven.

JESS. That's not going to cut it –

DENNIS. Wait wait wait –

MARYN. What.

DENNIS. Grimble looks at you – and you, you see this glint in his eye, he strums his lute – (*To* JESS.) – and I cast Bardic Inspiration.

DENNIS *gently plucks his guitar.*

MARYN. What does that mean?

DENNIS (*to* MARYN). That'll let you add a d6 to anything your roll.

He passes over a four-sided dice. MARYN *looks at it tentatively. Then rolls it.*

MARYN. Okay plus three. Ten.

JESS. The guard immediately passes out and starts snoring.

MILO. I kick the door down...

JESS. And... you enter the Office of the Magistrate. And there she is: her suit made of the finest silk in the city, her face set in stone-like neutrality. She puts down her quill.

I didn't realise I had a *meeting*.

MILO. This is not a meeting. This is an execution.

I point my sword at her neck.

JESS (*laughs*). I'm afraid if you hurt me, you'll be hounded through the city, strung up and killed.

MILO. We can deal with your guards.

JESS. She leans over her desk and smiles.
I'm not talking about guards, I'm talking about my citizens. They love me. And if you kill me, you will face the wrath of every single one of them.

MARYN. They'll understand when they realise you are an acolyte of the Nightmare King.

JESS. You think that matters to them? The economy is a success. Constables throughout the municipality. We've tightened our grip on elves entering the city – I'm sorry to say to you, wizard, we may have to check your documents on your way out.

MARYN. Fash.

MILO. Let's just kill her and search her things.

MARYN. Yep, okay.

MILO. Really?

MARYN. Yeah. It's okay to kill nazis.

DENNIS. Okay she's *right wing* but –

MARYN *snorts*.

Why don't we make a deal?

MARYN. We're not making a *deal*.

DENNIS. She cares about her reputation... there's leverage.

MARYN. *Ugh.*

MILO. That's got to be bad for your windpipe.

DENNIS. Let me have a go. Please?

JESS. Maryn?

MARYN *gestures: 'the floor is yours'*. DENNIS *clears his throat – he plays with total seriousness*.

DENNIS. Most Worthy Magistrate.

JESS. She warms to that.

DENNIS. I apologise for the haste of my companions. I see you are a smart woman. What does the Nightmare King offer you?

JESS. Protection. When his armies march, Grayport will be safe.

DENNIS. You tell us where the Nightmare King is. If we die, what's that to you? But if we defeat him, we keep you in state, and I will write your grace into an epic ballad –

MILO. Run her with a sword.

DENNIS. She knows where the Nightmare King is!

MARYN. She's a dictator!

DENNIS. Hang on – (*To* JESS.) *is* she a dictator?

JESS. She's elected.

DENNIS. *She's elected.* There you go.

MARYN. Hitler was elected.

DENNIS. We've broken in to a government building and threatened a democratically elected official at knife-point –

MARYN. She's a racist –

DENNIS. Well then… they knew what they were voting for –

MARYN. Did they?

DENNIS. What do you mean?

MARYN. The people of Grayport are – are – largely uneducated workers –

DENNIS. They're not idiots.

MARYN. Then why did they choose her?

DENNIS. I don't know, maybe there has been an influx of elves –

MARYN. *Oh my god.*

DENNIS. What, what?

MARYN. You voted Brexit didn't you.

DENNIS. What's that got to do with –

MILO (*reaching out to* DENNIS, *holding his arm*). It's okay, I would have voted Brexit.

DENNIS. I didn't vote [Brexit] – (*To* JESS.) Why are you grinning like that?

JESS. No reason.

DENNIS. Look just let me roll a Persuade check to see if it worked.

DENNIS *rolls. He rejoices.*

Natural twenty!

JESS. A crow flies past the window.

> She turns to you:
> Head to the mountains. Find the castle built into the highest peak. My lord has been very anxious about something hidden there. I don't know what it is, but he's intent that no one find it.

DENNIS. Thank you, Magistrate.

JESS. Let's stop there. Everyone may now... *level up!*

Everyone begins to pack up. MARYN*'s on her phone.*

MILO (*to* MARYN, *while clearing cups*). I could kill your boss. I would slice him up like steak.

MARYN. What are you doing?

MILO. I'm washing up.

MARYN. What?

> MILO *leaves, but has left a cup.* MARYN *heads to the kitchen.*

DENNIS. That was *amazing*. It's... it's very. God, I can't describe it. In my day it was just trolls and busty barmaids. Boys. Experimenting. This feels so –

He taps JESS*'s book.*

Now.

JESS. Well that's just fantasy, isn't it? Fantasy's not about *fantasy*. I'm going to stop saying fantasy.

DENNIS. You're good, Jess.

JESS. I'm not good.

DENNIS. You are. It's a great campaign.

> DENNIS *taps* JESS*'s notebook.*

Thanks for having me. It was a great session.

JESS. Keep playing.

DENNIS. What?

JESS. I want you to keep playing.

DENNIS. I can't be focusing on a long-term game right now. Easy to, you know –

DENNIS *makes a gesture: 'hyper-focus'.*

There's a lot of finance stuff at the moment. We've been – we were obviously a bit fucked by Covid so I'm still sorting that, and – well, I'm meant to be writing a novel...

JESS. You're writing a novel?

DENNIS. Yeah, I've got a friend from uni in publishing, and he's... he's asking for some pages –

JESS. What's it about?!

DENNIS. Elves and goblins and stuff. But my own *spin*. Anyway. So I... you know I –

JESS. That's more important.

DENNIS. I can think about it.

JESS *smiles, and packs up.*

MARYN. Anyway. Look. The point is, she's quit, and we have this – this – data entry role that's come up at the firm, it's not being advertised, and if you want to, I was thinking... I can put your name forward.

MILO. If you like.

MARYN. No. Look. Do you want me to do it? I'm happy to do it, but it means I'll have to be gunning for you in the meeting so, do you actually want me to?

MILO. I don't want it if it's nepotism.

MARYN. You'll still have to do an interview but do you want an interview.

MILO. Fine. Yeah I do. Fine.

MARYN. Okay. I will.

MILO *gets up.*

MILO. Right. Said I'd cook dinner for Mum but I don't know what I'm gonna make.

MILO *lingers in doorway.*

Is it hard to make dauphinoise potatoes?

MARYN. Yes.

JESS. Yes.

Beat.

MILO. Okay I'll just boil 'em.

MILO *goes.* JESS *has all her stuff ready.*

JESS (*to* MARYN). Are you coming?

MARYN. I'm actually going to stay and do a bit of work.

JESS. He's closing in a minute I think.

MARYN. I'm just wrapping up.
Say hi to Mum and Dad for me.

JESS *lingers for a beat, then goes.*

Long silence.

DENNIS. How's your job? Jessica mentioned you were having a bit of a hard time... long hours?

Beat.

MARYN. I just want you to have context.

Beat.

So you know what's happening.

Matt, Jess's brother, Milo's friend from school, died about six months ago.

So, anything. Every Thursday night. Anything she wanted to do with us, was the idea. And Matt loved these games so – so –

I just want you to be sensitive to that.

DENNIS. Did he kill himself or – or –

Beat.

Sorry. Idiot.

MARYN. It's six months next week. I overheard Jess wants you to keep playing. And I wanted to say, if you want to stop, now is a good time.

DENNIS. Mhm.

MARYN. Before it becomes a regular thing.

DENNIS. Got it.

MARYN. And it's not Jessica it's Jess, it's just Jess.

DENNIS. Okay.

MARYN. It's legally Jess. She doesn't like you calling her Jessica.

MARYN packs up.

DENNIS. How did you know him?

MARYN. We went out for a bit.

DENNIS. I'm / sorry.

MARYN. She told you I was having a hard time at work?

DENNIS. *Well.*

MARYN. She said that, she said 'having a hard time'?

DENNIS. Just that maybe it wasn't your calling, or –

MARYN. Well I'm not having a hard time, I'm getting loads done actually. And they've said they're giving me more responsibility now, so. It's good.

DENNIS. Okay. Cool.

MARYN. Goodnight.

DENNIS. Goodnight. Good game.

MARYN goes.

DENNIS *looks at Grimble's character sheet.*

BEV *knocks.* BEV *is fifty. She's in a white shirt, black trousers and heavy shoes. She does not know what to make of this place.*

DENNIS *stands up, reties his ponytail, and lets her in.*

Hello hello!

BEV. Hello!

DENNIS. This is it!

BEV. It really is...
You live here, then?

DENNIS. Downstairs. In the dungeon. Not the dungeon – basement. But – / loads of light.

BEV (*looking around*). High street's so dead, no Debenhams or Topshop anymore – but we've got this, round the back of Boots!
And it makes you money?

DENNIS. I wash my face with it.

DENNIS *pulls* BEV *out a chair. She sits, and sighs.*

BEV. Bloody hell.

DENNIS. What?

BEV. Nothing. Long day. Nothing is working like it used to. We're so behind.

DENNIS. How are you?

BEV. Just told you. Didn't I?

DENNIS. Do you want a drink?

BEV. I'm not drinking.

DENNIS. Forgot.

BEV *lifts her shoe.*

Floor's a bit sticky.

Beat. BEV *points to* DENNIS*'s guitar.*

BEV. I didn't know you played.

DENNIS. Oh, no. I don't. I don't.

BEV. Oh.

A long awkward silence. DENNIS *musters the courage.*

DENNIS. I do play.

BEV. What?

DENNIS. I do play. Would you like to hear a song?

BEV. Alright.

He puts the guitar on.

DENNIS (*bowing*). My lady.

He plays. It's beautiful.

The Nightmare King, with eyes of flame,
Beware his power, beware his name,
He waits within his cavern deep
To wrap the world in eternal sleep.

BEV *claps.*

I'm going to have a beer.

Beat.

BEV. Fuck it, fine. Yes please.

DENNIS *fetches her a beer.*

Naughty.

DENNIS. We could play something.

BEV. Oh I don't know. I'm not into all that... dragons and things, makes my head hurt.

DENNIS. You're saying to me you've never enjoyed a board game?

BEV. Well... I used to play a lot of Monopoly.

DENNIS *is defeated by this.*

What?

DENNIS. No *no*... we could play.

BEV. Not tonight.

DENNIS. You'd beat me, though.

She laughs.

BEV. No I wouldn't.

DENNIS. You would. You'd just keep winning.

BEV. Shut up.

DENNIS. And then I'd quit because I'd be so cross.
And then I'd lock the shop.
And then...

BEV. What.

DENNIS. We'd – um – we could –

They're close together now.

We could –

They kiss.

BEV. That was quick...

DENNIS. I like you.

BEV. I like you.

Do you remember, in that one session when we had to talk about our hidden talents, you spoke... what was it?

DENNIS. Elvish?

BEV. ...is it bad to say it turned me on a little bit?

DENNIS (*laughing a little*). Err... no, no.

I noticed.

Whispered in BEV*'s ear.*

Im'm at cín mercui herdir.

He bites her ear.

BEV. What does that mean?

DENNIS. Let's make a baby.

BEV. You're so lucky we can't.

They keep kissing. It gets a bit demonic.

DENNIS. I want to keep doing this.

They kiss some more.

BEV. We can. Just no… you know.
No games, alright?

DENNIS. No games.

Scene Three

JESS, DENNIS, MARYN *and* MILO *at the table.*

Eerie music playing from JESS's *laptop.*

JESS *is moving around the space, clutching her notebook. painting the picture.*

JESS. The castle stands in front of you. Encrusted in ice and covered with snow. Wind lashes against your face.

MILO. How big is it?

JESS. Bigger than the big Tesco.

MARYN (*checking with the group*). We go in? We go in.

JESS. You push through into the atrium of this grand old building.
Once lavishly furnished, now fallen from grace: dust blanketed everywhere, rusted pictures, rotting curtains. Huge stone steps twisting to the upper rooms. Icicles hanging from the bannister. On the balcony, the portrait of a handsome young knight.

ACT ONE, SCENE THREE

MARYN. I walk toward the portrait.

JESS. It's a painting of a boy. Brown hair, brown eyes, a faint smile on his lips.

MARYN. Do I know who it is?

JESS. Prince Faldir of Farshore.

MARYN. Anything else?

> MARYN *rolls*.

That's eighteen Perception.

JESS. There's something behind the painting.

MARYN. I get my fingers behind it.

JESS. The wall with the painting on it gives way, and swings open.

MILO. I step through…

MARYN. Careful, Milo.

MILO. I am being careful.

JESS. Inside, Maryn you'd recognise this… scattered around the room are all the calling cards of dark magic.

> Candles, spell books, dark gems, and on the floor, scrawled in chalk, a summoning circle.

> Floating above it is an object, encased in a blue kind of forcefield.

MARYN. What is it?

Beat.

JESS. A book.

> JESS *holds out her notebook*.

MILO. I pick it up.

> MILO *reaches for it but* JESS *moves it away*.

JESS. Forcefield.

DENNIS. I search the table for clues –

JESS. There's a note written hastily in ink on the table.

'The spirits will not leave me be. Tonight, I summon them here. Tonight, I face them.'

MARYN. *Oh.*

MILO. What?

MARYN. I don't think this guy is *connected to* the Nightmare King. I think this is the guy who *became* the Nightmare King.

DENNIS. I think we need that book. There's a reason he's protecting it.

JESS. The force around the book is a Ward of Protection. It's going to take about five minutes to break, and it's going to need two spellcasters. And if you fail, the book's gone forever.

MARYN. Grimble. Will you assist me?

DENNIS. If you trust me, Wizard.

MARYN. I trust you.
I put my hand on the Ward.

DENNIS. So do I.

MARYN. And we cast.

Silence, and total focus on the task. Then, out of nowhere.
JESS *makes a noise like a crow.*

MILO. What the fuck. Jess. Jesus.

JESS. You hear that noise outside the room.

MARYN. We can't leave the spell.

MILO. I step out into the atrium.

JESS. Below you... in the doorway, stands a huge black crow.
Beady black eyes darting in all directions.
It sees you.
And it begins to stalk toward you.

Each step it takes, stone collapses beneath its feet.

JESS *crows again.*

MILO. I grip my sword.

MARYN. Careful, Milo.

MILO. I lift myself onto the stairwell. (*To Maryn.*) I look at you.

Beat.

I blow you a kiss...

And I leap off, bringing my axe down on the monster.

MILO *rolls.*

...plus four... fourteen.

JESS. You miss, falling on the steps next to the bird, your axe lodging in the stonework.

MILO. Shit.

JESS. You take three Damage.

The bird rises up. Three, four times bigger than you. It lunges at you with its beak.

JESS *rolls.*

Nineteen.

MILO. Hit.

JESS *rolls again.*

Eight Damage.

MILO. Fuck!

JESS. Its beak rips through your shoulder, blood pours from it and you lose feeling in your left hand.

MILO. I get this look in my eye – like fire burning – finally go into a fucking Barbarian Rage, leap at the crow, and slice my sword right into its wing.

He rolls.

Eighteen.

JESS. Hit.

MARYN. Yes. Come on!

He rolls again.

MILO. Ten Damage.

DENNIS. There we go! Yes Milo!

JESS. Your axe cuts through the wing, it flails about and almost loses its balance.

MILO. Come at me mate.

MARYN. How's the Ward doing?

JESS. You're seconds off finishing the spell. There's time for the crow to attack once more. It screeches, and goes for you.

JESS *rolls*.

JESS. Twenty-two.

MILO. Hit.

JESS. How many hit points have you got left?

MILO. Nine.

JESS. Okay so there's a small chance this...

JESS *rolls again*.

Ten Damage.

Silence.

MILO. That's... that's all my Hit Points.

Beat.

JESS. Alright, so this is what's going to happen.

MILO. Don't sound so serious mate.

JESS. We enter Death Saving Throws. Milo. You're going to roll three d20. One after the other. If one of them is over ten. You survive. If you fail three times... you die.

JESS *places a dice in* MILO's *hand*.

MILO. Oh my god stress. Right.

MILO rolls one.

Four.

Beat.

JESS. Two more.

MILO. Ten for Daddy. Ten for Daddy.

He rolls a second.

Eight.

JESS. Last roll.

MILO. Fuck. Okay. Okay. Come on.

He kisses the dice in his hand.

Seven. Shit! *Shit!*

JESS (*intensely*). The crow plunges its beak through your heart, spearing you against the wall. It opens its mouth, tearing your chest apart. You gurgle, blood runs down your armour. Your vision becomes blurry. Your consciousness begins to slip away. You are about to die. Okay?

MILO. *Understood.*

JESS (*to* MARYN). The spell completes and the book falls into your hand.

JESS gives MARYN the notebook.

MARYN. R-r-rolling attack.

MARYN rolls. JESS nods.

I run into the room cast Magic Missile at fifth level for –

MARYN rolls.

– Fifteen Damage.

JESS. It falls to the ground, dead, burning.

MARYN. Er – I go to Wren and I cast, I cast –

JESS. You feel the darkness rising up through you, about to take hold –

MILO. Winglass... I always wanted to tell you... to tell you...

MARYN. What? What is it. Wren?

MILO. I touch your face. I look into your eyes. And then... I... I...

MILO dies. Everyone is drained. MILO has moved MARYN almost to tears. And then...

MILO starts laughing.

MARYN. Oh my god, fuck you.

DENNIS. That really [got me] – phew –

MILO (*pretending to pick up the phone*). Hello is that the – what's it called – we went with school –

MARYN. The / National Theatre?

MILO. Hello is that the National Theatre? No, I'm sorry, I'm completely fucking booked up.

MARYN. What were you gonna say?

MILO. Mystery.

MARYN. So smug.

MILO. Alright let's rewind and try that again.

JESS. What do you mean?

MILO. Well, I'll beat it this time.

JESS. We're not going again...

MILO. So... do I come back to life? How do we do this?

JESS. You're dead, Milo.

DENNIS. You know when I used to play you were just knocked out until the next quest –

MILO. Yeah – I could just be knocked out.

JESS. You're not knocked out... you got stabbed in the heart...

MARYN. Exactly so – that's why it makes more sense to just rewind.

Beat.

JESS. That's not how it works.

MARYN. Jess...

Beat.

Come on.

JESS. He can make a new character.

MARYN. Why are you being like this?

JESS. She's dead.

MARYN flicks through the playbook.

MARYN. Look, everyone just chill out, there's got to be something I can cast.

JESS. There's nothing you can cast, she's dead.

DENNIS. Jess –

JESS. *I'm the Dungeon Master.*

DENNIS. Okay, okay. Everyone's just got a bit heated... so we're all just going to cool down for a second...

MARYN (*pointing to a spell in the book*). What about Raise the Dead.

JESS. That lasts for thirty seconds. Do you want to bring her back for thirty seconds?

MARYN. Let me just find something.

JESS. There's nothing you can find.

MILO. Chill out.

JESS. If you're not playing by the rules what's the point in fucking doing this?

MARYN. I don't know, Jess. Babysitting? Do you think I haven't had anything better to do for the last three months? Don't you think there are other things I could be doing?

DENNIS. Okay. Everyone take a breath.

MARYN. I'm just saying, I'm trying to say –

JESS *grabs the notebook from* MARYN.

Oi.

JESS *goes.*

DENNIS. *Jess. Jess!*

DENNIS *puts the keys on the table and goes after her.*

Watch the shop.

MARYN. Ughhhh.

MILO. That was harsh.

MARYN. Yeah well. I didn't…

MILO. What?

Beat.

MARYN. I… didn't want you to die.

MARYN *picks at her nails. Silence.*

How did it go?

MILO. What?

MARYN. The interview.

Beat.

MILO. Oh. I didn't go.

I did some reading up about the company and it doesn't seem very ethical so I didn't go. What's the problem?

MARYN. *Of course it's not ethical. It's a city law firm.*

MILO. And the commute is like… quite long and…

MARYN. *MILO.*

MILO. *What?*

MARYN. *You can't just miss an interview!* I just set you up. I told my boss you were worth interviewing. I'm going to look like a fucking idiot.

MILO. Well I'm sorry that you chose to do that.

MARYN. What are you *doing*?!

MILO. It's my right to not go if I didn't want to go –

MARYN. You're sabotaging applications. The last job you had here you got fired for stealing –

MILO. Magic: The Gathering cards are expensive!

MARYN. You don't play Magic: The Gathering!

MILO. *So what?*

MARYN. Why don't you want this? I batted for you, there were other candidates who had degrees and very good CVs but I said no. I know this guy, I trust him –

MILO. *Why do you care?*

MARYN. Because you deserve it.

Out of the blue, MILO *tries to hold back tears.*

MILO. Oh. What's this? Sorry.

MARYN. Hey. Hey.

MILO *lets it out.*

MILO. No I don't.

MARYN *awkwardly embraces him.*

MILO *cries harder.*

MARYN. You've got to live your life. Matt wanted to be a writer. You're not taking anything away from him doing *data entry.*

MILO *recovers a little. Then cries again harder.*

Look...

MARYN *can't find the words.*

She sits there and fights off her own demons.

After a while, she instinctively gestures with her hands and mutters something.

MILO. What did you just – did you just –

MARYN. Nothing.

Beat.

MILO. Did you just cast a spell on me?

MARYN *shakes her head, and smiles.*

Beat.

MILO. What was it?

MARYN. ...Raise the Dead. Sixth level. Brings you back completely.

MILO *gasps, as if coming back to life. Acts it all out.*

I am alive. Thank you.

MARYN (*laughing*). Stop.

MILO. You saved me. Noble wizard. How can I repay you!

MARYN (*laughing*). *Stop stop stop.*

MILO. Why?

MARYN. I...

MILO. What is it?

MARYN. Well you were going to say something before you died and I wanted to know what it was.

MILO. It was nothing. Nothing.

MARYN. Are you sure?

Beat.

MILO. I wanted to say... you know.

MILO *takes a gamble*.

You are very handsome.

Beat.

MARYN. And you are beautiful, in your way.

MILO. If I said I wanted to hold you, would you let me?

MARYN (*straight back*). If I said I wanted to fuck you, would you let me?

MILO. Mm.

MARYN. What was that?

MILO. I would. I would.

MARYN. So would I.

MILO. I was going to say...

They kiss...

MARYN *almost falls off her chair.*

MARYN. I'm going to go.

MILO. Hey. No –

MARYN. Fuck.

MILO. Maryn –

DENNIS *comes back in.*

DENNIS. Maryn where are you –

MARYN. Work.

MARYN *goes.*

DENNIS. I can't find her.
You know we can't...

We can't have everyone shouting at each other like that.

DENNIS *goes over and to the counter and looks around.*
MILO *gathers his things.*

MILO (*darkly*). What are you doing?

DENNIS. Nothing.

MILO. You're checking if I've taken anything.

DENNIS. *No. Milo.*

MILO. I probably have.

DENNIS. Milo – get home safe.

> MILO *leaves. All the energy leaves* DENNIS. *He heads downstairs.*
>
> *After a while,* JESS *appears in the doorway clutching the notebook.*
>
> *She sits and reads it.*

Don't run off like that. Please?

JESS. Sorry.

DENNIS. Where did you go?

JESS. Palace Estates.

DENNIS. It's *dark* –

JESS. There's streetlights. They're not the new ones, they're the old ones, they're orange. The whole street goes orange...

DENNIS. What are you talking about?

> *Beat.*

JESS. I don't want to go home.

DENNIS. Well you have to. I already regret letting you stay last time.

JESS. I can't sleep.

DENNIS. You didn't sleep here either you just stayed up writing.

JESS. Please.

ACT ONE, SCENE THREE 55

DENNIS (*losing his temper*). I know that's – I'm sorry – but I don't want people thinking I'm a – [paedo] – do I? Maybe we should all stop playing for a bit.

JESS. What?

No.
I'm fine. We don't have to stop.

DENNIS. Look...

JESS. I won't do that ever again we don't have to stop.

DENNIS. Jess. Just.

JESS. *What?* I'm not gonna run off again – so –

DENNIS. I'm selling the shop.

JESS. Why? Is it the rent? We'll – we can do Kickstarter, we can post letters –

DENNIS. Listen –

JESS. It's important for the community – we'll get you on instagram, you're not on instagram, we'll do – we'll raise –

DENNIS. It's not really the rent – I mean I'm financially more solid *now* than I've been in a while –

JESS. Then what's the / problem?

DENNIS. It's all back in fashion, and if I played my cards right and put the work in –

JESS. Why don't you?

DENNIS. *Because it just doesn't do very much for me anymore.*

I used to gamble. It all got a bit *much* if I'm honest. You hate yourself, but you keep going. The same thing's happening here. I *love* this – (*He points to the table.*) but this (*Gestures at the shop.*)

I've had a good offer from Caffè Nero, Bev mentioned maybe me moving in, I want to write, maybe I'll make some new friends in town and –

JESS. We're your friends.

DENNIS. Yeah but...

JESS. But what?

DENNIS. You're sixteen, Jess.

JESS. Don't. *Don't.* Please.

DENNIS. It's disappointing. I get it.

JESS. Make a deal with me.

DENNIS. I'm not doing any *deals*.

JESS. *Don't close till we've finished the game.*

DENNIS. Don't say that.

JESS. I'll, I'll speed it up. I'll get things moving, but – let us get to the end.

DENNIS....

JESS (*scarily desperate*). Please. Please please please.
Who knows what adventures await?

ACT TWO
Scene One

BEV. Banker. *Banker*.

> JESS *snaps up.* DENNIS, BEV, MARYN *and* MILO *at the table too.*
>
> *They're playing Monopoly.* BEV, DENNIS *and* MILO *are drinking.* BEV*'s police uniform jacket draped over her chair.*

JESS. Sorry.

BEV. In her own world! I'd like to buy Fleet Street. Here you are…

> BEV *counts out her money and hands it to* JESS.

Then I'll take my turn.

> BEV *rolls. Then moves her piece.*

One. Two. Three. Four. Five.
Fleet Street. Okie dokie.

> BEV *counts out the money.*

One hundred, one-fifty, two-hundred, two-ten, two-twenty.

> BEV *passes dice to* DENNIS.

Your turn, love.

> DENNIS *rolls.*

DENNIS (*to* JESS). Can you move me five along please?

JESS. I just don't understand why we can't –

DENNIS. It's been four months of the Nightmare King, Jess, we can have a week off. Can you move me five along please?

> JESS *moves* DENNIS *along.*

I'd like to buy Old Kent Road.

MILO. Oh my god. Stop buying property. I'm absolutely fucked.

BEV. Language.

JESS. ...sixty quid.

DENNIS *pays*.

MILO. You hate Monopoly.

DENNIS (*sternly*). I love Monopoly, Milo.

He gives JESS *the money.* JESS *rolls*.

JESS. Eleven.

She makes her move.

BEV. So how do you all know each other?

MARYN. From school.

BEV. *From school.*

JESS *passes the dice to* MARYN *who takes her turn.*

(*To* JESS.) How old are you?

JESS. Sixteen.

BEV. You're still at school?

JESS. Yeah.

BEV. *Right*. And you two are a little older?

JESS. They're Matt's friends.

BEV. Who's Matt? *Boyfriend?*

DENNIS *lightly touches* BEV*'s hand.*

What?

JESS. Your turn Milo.

MILO *rolls*.

MILO. Fuck.

MARYN. *Just pay bail.*

MILO. I'm *not* paying bail. I'm getting out with a double.

He passes the dice to BEV.

BEV. Here we go again.

She rolls.

Double six!
Chance.

She draws.

Send a player of your choice straight to jail.

She unclips her handcuffs from her jacket.

Who's it going to be?

She waves them around.

DENNIS. Don't do it!

BEV. You're coming with me son! Or maybe it's not you.

BEV *moves the handcuffs around, and points at* MARYN.

Maybe it's you.

MARYN. *Fucking hell.*

Beat.

BEV. I'm just having a laugh.

DENNIS. I'll go to jail.

MARYN. I think for *you* to even be joking –

DENNIS. Maryn.

MARYN. What? What? It's – it's –

BEV. I didn't touch you.

MARYN. You can't just wave handcuffs about. Why do you even have those?

BEV. It was a joke!

MARYN. You don't get it do you.

Beat.

BEV. You know. Last week I had to visit the parents of that boy who got knocked off his scooter at the junction on Court Road. Yesterday, I helped a very brave abuse victim leave her house, and she could only do it because I was there.

MARYN. Where did she go afterwards? There's barely any emergency housing in the borough.

BEV. Just remember who's out there, and who's in here on their phone. My niece, her stories, it's bikini picture, Palestine, Trans Rights, bikini picture. What does she actually *do?*

DENNIS. Who wants a drink?

MARYN. I'm choosing not to engage with that, because you are avoiding the point, which is that there is strong evidence the police do net harm to every community you enter – more people in prison, more repeat offenders –

BEV (*quietly*). Grow up.

MARYN. What did you say?

BEV. Grow up love. Grow up.

MARYN. The first warning sign that you're in a cult is being faced with evidence and refusing to believe it. People like you can't look at yourselves in the fucking mirror.

DENNIS. Guys. Everyone's...

BEV. What? Everyone's what?

DENNIS. Everyone's valid.

MILO. This is so funny.

MARYN. / It's *not funny.*

BEV. *It's not funny.*

BEV is a little upset.

MARYN. Look... it's okay – just –

MARYN is almost crying too. It's all very raw.

BEV. Look at us. Sorry love I'm just a bit – a bit –

MARYN. I'm going to the loo.

MARYN gets up and goes.

DENNIS. Sorry.

MILO throws in his money.

MILO. I've lost anyway.

BEV. You can't quit halfway through. I'm trying to get to know you all. Dennis did girls' night.

DENNIS. I did.

MILO. I'm not going, I'm just not playing Monopoly.

BEV. What's wrong with Monopoly?!

MILO. It's like – My hell would be – You know in that movie when the guy has to play chess with Death? I'll have to play Monopoly Seventieth Anniversary Edition.

BEV (*to* JESS). What about you?

JESS. There's this variant of Monopoly called Longest Game Ever where you play until one person on the board owns every single property. It can go on for days.

BEV. But do you like it?

JESS. Not really.

DENNIS. Well look, we've got Risk, we've got Scrabble, we've got…

MILO. Those all make me want to kill myself.

DENNIS. Well – choose something, then.

JESS. We could play our game.

Beat.

DENNIS. No I don't think that's…

JESS. Why not?

BEV. What's your game?

JESS. We play Dungeons & Dragons.

BEV (*disbelief*). Oh no. (*To* DENNIS.) Is that what you're all up to? I thought it was just a club –

DENNIS. You knew I could speak Elvish.

MILO. You can speak Elvish?!

DENNIS. Daug angelenno.

MILO. What does that mean.

DENNIS. It means shut your mouth.

BEV. Were you embarrassed?

JESS. You were embarrassed?

DENNIS. I wasn't embarrassed.

JESS. Then let's play.

BEV. Go on.

DENNIS. Well there's loads of dice – so there's –

DENNIS *takes a pot of dice and pours it on the table*.

So this is a twenty-sided dice, and this is an eight-sided dice, and you have levels, basically, a character sheet with different stats, and –

JESS. It's a story.

DENNIS. Yeah, yeah. It's a story.

JESS. You play as a character. And you go on an adventure.

BEV (*to* DENNIS). Well who are you then?

DENNIS. I'm... I'm a dwarf.

BEV (*embarrassed*). I thought you couldn't say that anymore.

MARYN *comes back, recovered a little*.

DENNIS. No he's a, I'm a, *dwarven bard* –

JESS. Maryn introduce yourself.

MARYN.... She knows my name.

JESS. No, *introduce* yourself.

> MARYN *extends her hand, which* BEV *shakes.*

MARYN. I am Winglass, Wizard of the High Mountains, Chair of the Great University of Grathis, and Surveyor of the Seven Realms.

BEV. Lovely to meet you.

MARYN. A pleasure.

> MILO *offers his hand, and squeezes* BEV*'s.*

MILO. I am Wren, Daughter of the Kai, Warrior of the Great Wind.

BEV. A bit tight there, love.

MILO. I'm a warrior.
And, I'm pregnant.

BEV. You're pregnant?

MARYN. You're *pregnant*?

JESS. What?

MILO. I'm pregnant.

MARYN. Milo...

MILO. *What*? It's my choice whether I'm pregnant or not.

MARYN (*to* JESS). He can't be pregnant.

JESS. Well – you can be, you can be.

MILO. Yeah.

JESS. Whose baby is it?

MILO. *We just don't know.*

DENNIS. Guys –

JESS. They're all trying to stop the Nightmare King. Who's a baddie, who watches over everyone from the darkness, waiting to strike.

BEV. Ooh – like what's his name – oh god what's his name –

DENNIS. Lord Sauron?

BEV. Craig Revel Horwood.

MILO. Exactly like Craig Revel Horwood.

JESS. So you just have to decide who you want to be.

DENNIS. There's plenty of other things we can play –

BEV. *Jezebel.*

DENNIS. Sorry?

BEV. When I was little I had this game with my parents; when I was naughty, I think I got it from Sunday school, but I'd say I didn't do it. Jezebel did it. Used to pretend this other girl had snuck into the house. My Mum always said I picked up the name from church.
I'll be Jezebel.

JESS. Great. Jezebel. So in our world she has to be like –

BEV. Oh, she has to be a dragon.

JESS. No just a –

DENNIS. A medieval person.

BEV. Well then she's a… what is she…

JESS. Well the classes are… Wizard, Barbarian, Paladin, Rogue –

BEV. What's a Rogue?

JESS. Like a thief.

BEV. She's that. She's a thief.

JESS. So what, she…

ACT TWO, SCENE ONE 65

BEV. She picks pockets. She sells black-market goods in back alleys... Maybe she's even... a hired assassin.

DENNIS. You're good at this.

BEV. No I'm not, shut up.

JESS. Let's say you're in the forest.

BEV. Has it started?

DENNIS. Yeah, you're playing right now. You're in the forest.

BEV. Sorry! I'm in the forest.

JESS. You're camping with stolen goods. And you hear a rustle in the trees.

BEV. Oh, and it's a bear!

JESS. No – so – I decide what there is.

BEV. I see.

JESS. Do you approach the rustling?

BEV. ...I approach.

JESS. A knight in heavy armour bursts out of the undergrowth...

BEV. Ooh!

JESS. He raises his sword and points it at you. Thief!

BEV. Right. *Right.*
And what do I do?

DENNIS. Well you have to fight him, love...

BEV. And how do I do that?

DENNIS. Say what you want to do to him.

BEV. I don't know... give him a biff?

MILO. *Give him a biff?*

DENNIS. You've got to, you know, slice him with your sword. Or throw a knife at him or...

BEV. I just want to – can't I just magic him away on a holiday?

MARYN. He's an agent of the Nightmare King. You need to… you know. Kill him.

JESS *rolls*.

JESS. He swipes his sword across you for…

JESS *rolls again*.

Six Damage. He cuts your face.

BEV. Bastard!

JESS. What are you going to do?

BEV. I'm going to restrain him.

JESS. Roll.

BEV *rolls*.

BEV. Nineteen. Is that good?

JESS. That's great. You pull him down. Roll Damage.

JESS *passes a different dice*. BEV *rolls*.

BEV. One.

JESS. You manage to pin him down for a second. You get one punch in –

JESS *rolls*.

But then he slams you back against the tree.

He takes his knife and puts it to your throat.

Prepare to die.

And then there's a – a – high wind.

And these crows begin to caw.

And you feel the Dark Lord's *presence around you*. Every joint in your body freezes over. Your head starts to hurt. Figures bleed out of the trees.

DENNIS. Jess…

JESS. And they surround you – they've got their swords pointed at you – they're going to kill you, here in the forest.

DENNIS. *Jess*.

JESS. What?

DENNIS. You've given her a flavour.

JESS. Do you want to play with us? You could come. It's every Thursday night.

BEV. Oh I'd – I'd have to see –

DENNIS. *Jess*.

JESS. What?

DENNIS. We're meant to be wrapping this in the next few weeks we're not making it longer.

JESS. It won't take longer. It's just a new person. It's not going to take *longer*.

It's just a couple more, a couple more sessions.

MARYN. Jess.

JESS. What?

MARYN. You're talking a bit fast, again.

JESS. Oh. Sorry.

MARYN. It's okay.

JESS. I didn't mean to. Sorry.

DENNIS *starts to pack up Monopoly.*

BEV. Let me help.

DENNIS. I can do it.

BEV. Don't be silly. (*To* JESS.) You sort out the money I can never work that out –

Then, MARYN *grabs* MILO *and walks him over to the corner of the room.*

MARYN. Okay, look. This pregnant thing. I don't like it.

MILO. What about it?

MARYN. Well –

MILO. It's a *character beat*.

MARYN. You should have asked me.

MILO. It's not your decision.

MARYN. Can we just stop whatever this is.

MILO. Whatever what is?

MARYN. This is.

MILO. It is what it is.

MARYN. Seriously. Stop.

MARYN goes. MILO packs up his stuff, deflated.

BEV. DeSilva?

JESS. What?

BEV. Is that your last name? Was Matthew DeSilva was your brother?

JESS. How do you... [know?]

BEV. I was called in once or twice. They'd get us out because he'd be running through Churchill Gardens away from a – what was it?

JESS. A giant crow.

You never knew when it was going to happen.

BEV. He'd always ask for paper.

JESS. Yeah.

BEV. If we had to hold him, or we were waiting for your parents. He'd always be scribbling.

JESS. I mean my whole family is – Dad's obsessed with Tolkien. Mum's favourite writer is Octavia Butler. They always said we should write our ideas down, keep journals. I never really did it but but he did. His ideas were amazing.

ACT TWO, SCENE ONE 69

Except sometimes they weren't ideas, you know they were, for him they were real. We weren't meant to talk about it, Mum didn't want people thinking it was their fault, you know, with all the books, the fantasy –

BEV. Was that why?

JESS. No. No. It's genetic. My mum's dad. He saw nazis everywhere, apparently.

BEV. I hope you're looking after yourself.

JESS. I am.

MILO. Oi, Jess. You coming? The depression ice cream place is still open...

JESS *eyes* BEV.

JESS. Will you play?

BEV. I'll think about it.

BEV *writes a number down on her pad.*

Call me if you need anything.

JESS. Thanks.

MILO (*calling*). *JESS!*

JESS. Coming!

JESS *joins* MILO.

Why are we going to the depression ice cream place?

MILO. Because I'm depressed.

JESS *and* MILO *go.* DENNIS *finally fits the box in the shelf.*

DENNIS. Why'd you say you'd –

BEV. What?

DENNIS. She drags it out. Side quests – people in danger – She's just looking for reasons to keep it going. Don't say you're playing.

BEV. Why not just pick a day and tell her you're closing?

DENNIS. I... can't do that.

BEV. Why not?

DENNIS. What if we don't finish. She'd –

BEV. If you don't finish you don't finish.

DENNIS. But we should finish. It's tough for her, Bev.

BEV. *She's* dragging it out?

DENNIS. I mean – partly –

BEV. Have you approved the sale?

DENNIS. I'm hammering out the details, it's got to work for me, I can't just give this place away.

BEV. And do you have a move in date yet?

DENNIS. Bev.

BEV. You won't say when you're moving in. You won't book a holiday.

DENNIS. You're not getting it.

BEV. What am I not getting.

DENNIS. You're... you're...

BEV. You don't want to, do you?

DENNIS. Just... I keep thinking. *What's the rush?*

BEV. Come on Dennis, you're not a wizard! Or a dwarf! Or whatever! You're a fifty-five-year-old man! You spend all your time with children.

DENNIS. And you wish you'd *had children*. So we're both... we're both...

DENNIS *gives up. Beat.*

BEV (*to herself*). Don't go out with someone you met at fucking Gamblers Anonymous.

DENNIS. Bev –

BEV *leaves*.

DENNIS *sits at the table. He rests his forehead on it. He runs his fingers along it…*

Scene Two

DENNIS, MILO, MARYN *and* BEV *at the table*.

MARYN. Chai latte.

DENNIS (*his mind somewhere else*). I don't know about this.

MILO. An ale, Grimble!

DENNIS. I really don't know about this.

BEV. I'd love a white wine.

DENNIS. I'll try my best.

DENNIS *goes*.

MILO. Oi. Cheer up.

MARYN. Why?

MILO. You got a promotion!

MARYN. Yeah.

MILO. What?

MARYN. I'm swamped.

MILO. Then quit!

MARYN. Milo, just stop. Please. Not today.

MARYN *turns to* BEV. *Smiles. Can't talk to her. Turns back to* MILO.

Do you remember *Chrono Trigger*?

MILO. Kind of.

MARYN (*very fast*). It was the only game my dad had on his Super Nintendo and I don't play games but when he was away on work once when I was ten I played it all weekend and you know how there's that robot called Robo?

And he starts planting these trees and you come back four hundred years later and there's a whole forest there and he spent four hundred years just looking after the trees. I think it's meant to be this beautiful moment but I found it sort of terrifying.

The *patience*.

I always think I'm running out of time.

DENNIS *returns with the drinks. He hands* BEV *the wine*.

DENNIS. Give it a taste. It's screw top so it's not corked but I'm still suspicious of it.

BEV. You're shaking.

DENNIS. I'm not.

JESS *has entered*.

Hey, Jess.

DENNIS *hands* JESS *a mug*.

Hot choc.

JESS. Er… thanks.

MILO. Well met, Warrior!

JESS. Hi Milo…

MARYN. Welcome, Dungeon Master!

DENNIS. We are excited!

Beat.

JESS. For what?

DENNIS. We thought we might finish tonight.

JESS. Oh. Well don't worry, we're not.

Beat.

MARYN. Well we're close, that's what we thought.

JESS. You've still got to find the stronghold, there's towns to pass through – there's, there's some battles –

We're not finishing tonight. Shall we –

DENNIS. Okay. Right. Yeah. So.

MARYN. Um.

JESS. *What?*

DENNIS. *Tonight's the last night.*

Beat.

JESS. I just said it's not.

DENNIS. They're coming in on Saturday, moving everything out.

JESS. There's still loads to do.

MARYN. Jess.

JESS. We had a deal.

DENNIS. I know.

JESS. *We're not finished.*

MARYN. Dennis has to close, Milo's got to sort his fucking life out.

MILO. Oi.

MARYN. I mean – so do I. We can't keep doing this.

JESS. He doesn't have to close.

BEV. Leave the party while you're having fun.

Beat.

JESS. You're making him do it.

BEV. Hang on.

JESS. Ever since you started playing –

BEV. *You* asked me to play.

DENNIS. No one is making me do anything. I want to close.

JESS. Why didn't you tell me?

MARYN. Jess.

JESS. Why.

MARYN. Because –

JESS. You should have said.

DENNIS. I have. You're not *listening*.

JESS *takes a step back*.

And, it's not... *you're not*...

JESS. What?

BEV. It's not always healthy, is what he's trying to say.

JESS. It's the one nice thing. Don't... don't... [ruin it.]

DENNIS. What?

JESS. If you hate it this much, I'll just go.

JESS *turns to leave*.

MILO. We love it. We love it. And we want to know what happens in the end!

JESS. We're not ready. It's got to finish when it feels – it's got to feel right.

MILO. You are ready. You've got it all there in your head.

JESS. But there isn't an ending.

MARYN. You've done so much work on this, *there's an ending*.

JESS. There isn't an ending.

DENNIS. Come on, Jess, you're being –

ACT TWO, SCENE TWO   75

JESS. There isn't an ending because he didn't write one.

Beat.

DENNIS. But it's your… your…

JESS. It's not. It's his.

> JESS *puts the book down on the table.*

He wrote it. He wrote it all.

And it doesn't have an ending.

Silence.

No one wants to talk about him. No one ever wants to talk about him.

MARYN. Why do you think we're here?

JESS. You have to be. You just feel guilty. You both just feel guilty.

Why didn't you go to the funeral?

MARYN. I – I wanted to.

JESS. I waited for you at the door…

MARYN. Of course that's his book. Fuck. Of course.

> MILO *reaches out to touch the notebook.*

JESS (*she holds the notebook tight*). Mum didn't want him to have it because – he'd write stuff he'd seen, and he'd get worse – we took away his books, we weren't meant to talk about it, but it was all he wanted in the hospital so I brought it.

We had lunch. He was laughing, and asking about you guys, and fussing with his hair, and I gave it to him, and I went and, two hours later –

A long pause.

Inside I wrote 'You'll be home soon.'

Then, DENNIS *walks off. Silence.* MARYN *is crying to herself.*

And… DENNIS *pushes on a huge chest. He opens it.*

DENNIS. I used to LARP.

BEV. What's LARP?

DENNIS. Live Action Role Play, you – you –

MILO. You dress up and go to a big field and pretend to be at war with middle-aged men.

BEV. Like historical reenactment?

DENNIS. No, like the Battle for Minas Tirith. I wouldn't do anything *real*.

He opens the box. He takes out a bright red doublet... and puts it on. Then takes his guitar.

I believe it is time to face the Nightmare King.

JESS *looks at him. She smiles just a little.*

JESS *takes out a huge broadsword. A schoolgirl with Excalibur.*

Careful with that. It's from the 1987 shoot of *Willow*.

Starring Warwick Davis.

He's signed it.

JESS *passes it to* BEV, *who immediately drops it.*

Fucking hell.

The players dress up.

MILO *in plastic armour and blue facepaint.*

MARYN *in a huge wizard hat, and clutching a wooden staff.*

BEV *in a cloak with daggers strapped around her waist.*

MILO. Are you alright?

MARYN. I'm fine, Milo.

JESS. Do the speech.

DENNIS. What?

JESS. I want to hear the speech.

DENNIS. Oh don't say that...

It makes it feel like it's the last time.

MARYN. It *is* the last time!

BEV. Well go on then, do the bloody speech!

DENNIS *reluctantly gets up.*

DENNIS. So we used to... when we first opened... Anyway.

MILO. Wait wait wait.

MILO *shoves a pillow under his belly.*

MARYN. No. *Take that out.*

MILO. *No.*

MARYN *tries to pull it out,* MILO *keeps it where it is.*

Stop! Get off!

MARYN. I don't want you wearing it.

MILO. You're scaring the baby.

BEV. Control yourselves.

MARYN. *Milo.*

DENNIS *turns away, plucks his guitar in a rhythm.*

The room goes quiet.

Then he explodes:

DENNIS. WELCOME TO WARBOAR. I AM YOUR GUIDE TO THE WORLD OF FANTASY GAMING.

AS YOU SCRAMBLE THROUGH TOMBS, I WILL PROVIDE SUSTENANCE, AS YOU BATTLE MONSTERS, I WILL BRING YOU POTIONS, AND WHEN YOU TIRE OF YOUR JOURNEY, I WILL OFFER UP NEW WORLDS.

Then hushed, intense:

This is not a refuge. This is not an escape. The exercise of fantasy is to imagine other ways of life. Without understanding how others might live, I ask you, how will we ever understand ourselves? As you embark. Be judicious. Be clever. And band together. You never know what you might discover.

WHO KNOWS WHAT ADVENTURES AWAIT?

The fantasy consumes them. JESS *takes out the notebook.*

She reads the last few pages. Shuts it. She places it on the table.

JESS. You are heading North.
The further you go, the shorter the days.
Soon they evaporate completely, but you walk on through the dark.

Past forests and rivers, cities and farmland. The people are quiet. The doors are locked. The taverns are empty.

You come to a road sign.

Above it, a goblin's head is mounted on a spike. You recognise its face.

You've felt a numbness, ever since you embarked. The world has lost its colour. You are breathless. Weak. And sick.

Your dreams are full of crows, picking at the corners of your head.

You wake, still in the night of these Northern Realms.

There's barely any food left, little water.

You walk on. Nearing the stronghold. According to the map, it should be in the mountains beyond.

Beat.

DENNIS. Well, we press on.

JESS. You step into a valley, and you are met with a wall of fog. Thick and impenetrable.

ACT TWO, SCENE TWO 79

MARYN. We step in.

JESS. You lose all sense of direction in here. You can't see the hands in front of your face.

MARYN. I cast Dispel Magic, cancelling any spellcasting in a ten metre radius.

JESS. The fog clears.

MILO. What is there, then?

JESS. At the end of the valley, there's a sheer rock face.

You follow it along, and you find a passage, leading down into the heart of the mountain.

DENNIS. We go through it, right? We go through it.

JESS. It's narrow. There are sharp rocks jutting out on either side.

DENNIS. We go *through*.

JESS. You slice open your flesh on these rocks. Everyone takes five Damage.

MILO. Ooh, brutal.

JESS. You emerge into... well it's not a room. A space. Endless darkness... stars beyond. A door at the other side, glowing. of the room, glowing.

MARYN. Then we go to it –

JESS. In between you and the door is a pool of black liquid. And there is a ferryman. His face is gaunt. His skin a peeling moss. A servant of the Nightmare.

He awaits you.

DENNIS. Then I step onto the boat.

JESS *shakes her head*.

JESS. The boat starts to sink the moment your feet touch the bow.

DENNIS. I step back off.

JESS. The boat rises.

MARYN. What do you need?

JESS. He points to a rock by the shore, stained with blood. Beside it: a rusted axe.

Sacrifice.

A chill washes over them.

BEV. Well it should be me.

DENNIS. We're not killing you.

BEV. Well how else are you getting across? I – I don't even really like this game.
I don't mean – I do like it. I like you all I just –

DENNIS. I'll do it.

BEV. Absolutely not.

MILO. Thank you, Dennis. I know that is hard, but it's for the good of the campaign.

MARYN. Why are you playing by the rules?

MARYN *grabs the sword.*

I grab the Ferryman.

JESS. Oh!

MARYN. I kick him down over the rock. And I attack, sixteen plus two, eighteeen –

JESS. Hit.

MARYN. Ten Damage.

JESS. You got him. How do you want to do this?

MARYN. I swipe at his head. It connects, gliding through the sinews, and his head falls into the water. Blood pumps out of his neck and onto the rock.

MILO. That was –

MARYN. What?

MILO. That was quite hot.

MARYN. I step onto the boat.

JESS. It takes your weight.

MILO. Wren steps on. I hope it takes us all.

MILO *rubs his stomach.*

MARYN. Just take it out.

MILO. What am I gonna do, give birth in the boat?

DENNIS (*to* BEV). With me.

BEV. Thank you, kind soul.

JESS. You sail across the dark, and approach the door, runes around it glowing white.

DENNIS. We open the door.

JESS. You step through into a cavern. The door slams shut behind you.

JESS *crows.*

MILO. Really?

JESS. It steps toward you. Stitched together. Dripping that black liquid. It stalks toward you.

MILO. I don't want this.

JESS. It lunges at Jezebel, plunging its beak into her side, for fifteen Damage.

BEV. Bloody hell. That's me almost done.

JESS. It goes for you next, swiping at you with its wing, cutting you across the chest for twenty-one Damage.

MILO. I'm going for this bastard.

MARYN. Don't. You're already hurt.

MILO. I don't need protecting.

MARYN. Yes you do!

   JESS *crows again.*

   I run to the passage on the other side. I drag her with me.

JESS. Roll Dexterity.

   MARYN *rolls.*

MARYN. Five. Shit.

JESS. It turns. It knocks you both back. Tears through your flesh with its talons. Twenty-six Damage.

DENNIS. This isn't fair, Jess. You're not giving us a chance to defend.

JESS. It's in the book.
Winglass, it lifts its beak over you, and it pecks at your eyes, its huge beak driving in your face –

   DENNIS *strums his guitar and sings:*

DENNIS. *The Nightmare King, with eyes of flame,*
Beware his power, beware his name,

JESS. What are you doing?

DENNIS Distracting it.
He waits within his cavern deep
To wrap the world in eternal sleep.

   I cast Bardic Inspiration, sixth level, adding a d8 to every Dexterity roll.

   Go, everyone. Go.

JESS. It turns to Grimble. And closes its beak around his neck.

BEV. Oh, *love.*

MILO. Dennis!

DENNIS. **Go.**

MARYN. We head to the passage.

BEV. You don't have to – I can –

DENNIS. Just. Go.

    JESS *rolls. She can't believe it.*

JESS. Thirty two Damage.

DENNIS. I'm dead.

    DENNIS *and* JESS *stare at each other.*

    I'm. Dead.

MARYN. We're through the passage.

JESS. I didn't say you were through the passage yet.

MARYN. We're through the passage. What is here?

JESS. You're in a corridor. A corridor lined with torches.

MARYN. We walk down it. What's at the end?

    Beat.

    Jess, what's at the end.

JESS. A door.

MARYN. I open it.

JESS. It's locked.

MARYN. Okay…

MILO. I slam into it with my shoulder.

JESS. It doesn't open.

MARYN. I pull the handle hard.

JESS. It's not going to work.

MARYN. Hey…

JESS. It *doesn't work.*

    JESS *goes quiet.*

    BEV *knocks on the table.*

    The door creaks open.

BEV. I go inside.

JESS. You are in his throne room.

And...

He's there.

A cloak of black feathers, on his head a crown.

And he says. He says...

JESS is really struggling here.

BEV. Everything alright?

JESS. I'm fine.
I've been waiting for you.

BEV. I walk toward him.

JESS. He lifts a finger.

A sharp pain stings your entire body as you feel the blood freeze in your arteries.

You take twenty Damage.

DENNIS. Christ.

BEV. I get up. I go again.

JESS. I don't want to hurt you.

BEV. What else am I going to do?

JESS. Your heart begins to freeze over. Another twenty Damage.

BEV. I get up –

MARYN. Wait. Wait. Think about it. There's got to be a way to –

JESS. He takes a single step toward you, Wren. He lifts a finger... and launches Call Lightning.

JESS rolls.

Thirty-six Damage –

MARYN. I jump in front of the magic.

ACT TWO, SCENE TWO   85

MILO. No –

JESS. Are you *sure* Maryn?

MARYN. Yes of course I'm sure!

JESS. You're struck by lightning for thirty-six hit points.

MARYN. I attack.

> MARYN *rolls*.

Seventeen.

JESS. That's a hit. Roll Damage.

MILO. Maryn. Oi, *MARYN*.

MARYN. Rolling damage.

> MILO *lifts the sword*.

MILO. Put the dice down.

MARYN. What the fuck are you doing!

MILO. *I'm* attacking.

MARYN. Milo.

MILO. I'm not letting you die.

MARYN. Oh god! I'm not going anywhere Milo, okay! I'm not going anywhere.

> MILO *hears this, and something in him lets go*.

JESS. He prepares another spell, fire gathering in his fingertips.

MARYN. Hang on –

DENNIS. Jess – you can't just keep attacking –

JESS. This is his level, these are his stats, this is how many moves he gets per round. You're on the floor now, you're covered in blood, he walks toward you, his fingers flickering with lightning, his laugh echoing around the cavern.

Every flame will snuff out. Every light will turn black.

MARYN. There's got to be something. He wouldn't write it like this.

JESS. He did.

MARYN. He wouldn't Jess.

JESS. He *did*.

MARYN. There'd be a way out. There'd be a way to stop him.

DENNIS. Well, there's the book.

MILO (*urgent*). Well what do we do with it?

MARYN *flicks through her spell sheet –*

MARYN. Maybe there's something I can cast –

DENNIS (*calmly*). I don't think *we* can do anything. I don't think we're who he left it for.

Tell your story, Jess. Don't get lost in his.

JESS *thinks*.

JESS. You stand there covered in blood, barely breathing, no strength to go on...

He towers above you... and for a second, a fraction of a second, the shadows part, and you see his face. Not the Nightmare, the Prince.

He sees you all.

MARYN. There you are.

JESS *looks at the adventuring party. And she makes a decision.*

With immense effort... she tears the book in half. She closes her eyes.

JESS. There is a scream from the depths of the earth.

Shadows *splinter* from the Nightmare King and draw into the ground. He lifts up into the sky, and the darkness leaves him. The Prince falls on the cold stone.

And he's dead. No more shadows. Only a few scars.

JESS *hugs* DENNIS.

DENNIS. I love you.

JESS. I love you too.

BEV. Wow.

MILO. What?

BEV. You can really *see it in your head*, can't you?
All of it.

Scene Three

Caffè Nero, Bromley, BR1.

JESS *is sat at the table, writing.* DENNIS *stands next to her.*

DENNIS. Can I get you anything? Hot chocolate?

JESS. Yes please.

> DENNIS *heads to the counter.* JESS *wraps up her notes.*
>
> DENNIS *returns.*

DENNIS. Er. He'll bring it over.

JESS. It's so weird, it's the exact same layout.

DENNIS. *I know.* Took everything I could to not go and make it myself. Done a bit of a lazy job if you asked me. There's a bit of paint mismatch... How was the memorial?

JESS. It was good. I did a speech. It was in the Masonic Lodge in Sydenham so I snuck in secret messages for him – thought it was appropriate.

DENNIS. Like what?

JESS. Oh like when I blinked twice it meant I know this bit's not true but Mum wants me to say it. When I tapped the podium with my little finger it was like, warning, there's an embarrassing story about you coming.
And when I scratched my ear it meant...

DENNIS. What did it mean?

JESS *just smiles knowingly.*

JESS. How's the book going.

DENNIS. I'm not writing a book.

JESS. Seriously?

DENNIS. I'm not writing a book.

JESS. What the fuck, Dennis!

DENNIS. Sorry.

JESS. That's so disappointing. Why did you say you were writing a book!

DENNIS. *Don't.*

JESS. *Why?*

DENNIS. Oh bloody hell... I was saying it to impress you.

JESS. Impress me?

DENNIS. Well – I think there was a bit of me that's, yeah, jealous of you still so –

JESS. Jealous?

DENNIS. Last few years there's this voice at the back of my head, you know. And I wonder sometimes if I wasted my energy. It's all ahead of you. I spent most of my life playing bloody games.

JESS. What's wrong with that?

DENNIS. Maybe you're right. Fantasists run the bloody world.

JESS. I wish fantasists ran the world.

DENNIS *laughs.*

DENNIS. *How na aglon i anand.*

JESS. What's that? 'How to keep?'

DENNIS. Pass. How to pass the time. My whole life it's been: how to pass the time.

ACT TWO, SCENE THREE

MILO *appears in Caffè Nero uniform and hands over two drinks.*

MILO. One hot choc, one decaf amo.

JESS. Thanks mate.

MILO. I'll be one minute, my *gorgeous* manager wants me to get in a few more orders before I'm off.

MARYN *enters. New hair. Blue or green or both.*

JESS. New hair.

MARYN. Yes, well work don't like it but fuck work.

DENNIS. Hello mate.

MARYN. So I've got two hours, then I'm going to a very important Bromley Progressive Alliance meeting, we're voting for Treasurer and I'm ahead in the polls.

JESS. You ran *polls*?

MARYN. I sent round a fake email pretending to be an independent body researching local activist groups. I'm also running a light defamation campaign. *What?* Who says I'm a good person?

I thought you did a good speech at the... thing.

JESS. So did I.

BEV *enters dressed as Jezebel – in a cloak, hood, boots and daggers.*

A moment of suspension...

Then:

What are you wearing?

BEV. We're not... it's not... we're not dressing up again?

DENNIS. Why would we be – ?

BEV. Milo sent me an email saying we were all... *oh my god that little shit.*

MILO *enters. He pisses himself laughing.*

MILO. Oh my god, I can't believe you fell for it –

BEV. If someone recognises me I'm in so much trouble.

BEV *takes her hood off.*

Does this look normal? Do I look normal?

DENNIS. I think you look rather fetching.

BEV. Oh shut up.

MILO. Hey.

MARYN *hugs* MILO.

MARYN. Hello mate.

They sit around the table.

We could start again. We could play something else. Whatever. Just to say.

JESS. I think we're good to keep going.

JESS *cracks open a new notebook.*

Dennis.

DENNIS.... Yes?

JESS *plays some high stakes music from her laptop.*

JESS. Could you roll me a Death Saving Throw.

JESS *slides him a dice.*

DENNIS *shakes the dice. Everyone leans in.*

He rolls.

Five. Nope.

Rolls again.

Two.

MILO. Come on come on come on come on.

Rolls again.

DENNIS. Natural twenty.

MILO. YES MATE!

DENNIS. I'm alive! I'm alive!

JESS. So it's two months later. You guys saved the realm, obviously, so you got given a medals and gold and all that. And, and... where are you now?

DENNIS. Grimble and Jezebel have moved in together.

BEV. Because Grimble stopped being a cunt.

DENNIS. And he's paying half the council tax.

JESS. What does your house look like?

DENNIS. Well it's not a house, it's a castle.

BEV. Oh yeah. Loads of square footage.

DENNIS. Big, overgrown garden. Vines climbing up the bricks. Crossbows lining the battlements.

BEV. And a spa.

DENNIS. And secret passageways built by an ancient king.

BEV. And it's really close to the shops.

MARYN. We visit, obviously.

MILO. Yeah, and one afternoon Wren...

MILO launches into some incredibly convincing contractions breathing techniques.

MARYN. Shhh. Oh my god. Shhh.

BEV. This is incredibly convincing.

MILO. I've been watching videos.

DENNIS. Oh my god.

MILO. **Oooh. She's a big one.**

JESS. And – and – she's born. Milo. She's born.

MARYN. Do you want me to...

MILO. No no. It's not yours. She is the child of a wandering knight. I'm a single mum.

MARYN. Okay.

MILO. What? My mum did it.

JESS. You hold her. And she's the most beautiful thing you've ever seen, obviously... and... and...

MARYN. Um. I'm going to ask something.

What happened to the Nightmare King? The... Prince?

JESS. Oh –

MARYN. We don't have to –

JESS. No, no, it's good.

You send him off.

You lay him on a pyre, demons washed away, scars on his cheeks.

The sky is a dying pink.
You cast a gentle spark, and the pyre lights.
The smoke travels over the mountain.

You breathe in the evening air.

Look off toward the sea.
And you think to yourselves...

(*Teasing, to* DENNIS.) Who knows what adventures await?

The End.

www.nickhernbooks.co.uk

@nickhernbooks